SE   '15

American Indian Homes

Plank Houses

by Riley Flynn

CAPSTONE PRESS
a capstone imprint

First Facts are published by Capstone Press,
1710 Roe Crest Drive, North Mankato, Minnesota 56003
www.capstonepub.com

Library of Congress Cataloging-in-Publication Data
Flynn, Riley.
  Plank houses / by Riley Flynn.
      pages cm. — (First facts. American Indian homes)
  Includes bibliographical references and index.
  Summary: "Informative, engaging text and vivid photos introduce readers to American
Indian plank houses"— Provided by publisher.
  ISBN 978-1-4914-2055-3 (library binding)
  ISBN 978-1-4914-2241-0 (paperback)
  ISBN 978-1-4914-2261-8 (eBook PDF)
1. Indians of North America—Dwellings—Northwest Coast of North America. 2. Plank
houses—Northwest Coast of North America. I. Title.
  E78.N79F59 2015
  392.3'608997--dc23

                                              2014025809

Editorial Credits
Anna Butzer, editor; Sarah Bennett, designer; Tracy Cummins, media researcher;
Gene Bentdahl, production specialist

Photo Credits
Alamy: Gary Crabbe/Enlightened Images, Front Cover, 13; Bridgeman Images: Werner
Forman Archive, 5, Wood Ronsaville Harlin Inc. USA, 17; Capstone Press, 6; Corbis: Edward S.
Curtis, 7, Joel W. Rogers, 11, Marilyn Angel Wynn/Nativestock Pictures, 15, 19; Getty Images:
Marilyn Angel Wynn, 1; Shutterstock: chungking, 9, Josef Hanus, 21, marchello74, Back
Cover, Design Element; SuperStock: Frank Pali/age fotostock, 3.

Printed in the United States of America in North Mankato, Minnesota.
092014   008482CGS15

Table of Contents

Chapter 1

What Is a Plank House?

Plank houses are made of wide boards called planks. American Indians built and lived in plank houses. The houses looked like large rectangular or square boxes. They had one door and no windows.

Plank houses varied in size. Smaller plank houses were 40 to 60 feet (12 to 18 meters) long. Larger homes were as long as 100 feet (30 m).

totem pole—a pole
carved and painted with
animals and other objects
that represent a family

Chapter 2

Who Lived in a Plank House?

American Indians of the Northwest Coast lived in plank houses. These **tribes** included the Chinook, Haida, and Tlingit. Many related families lived together in a plank house.

Today American Indians still use a few of these traditional homes. They build and use plank houses for community centers.

Where the Indians of the Northwest Coast Lived »

1. Canada
2. United States
3. Where the Indians of the Northwest Coast Lived
4. Pacific Ocean

tribe—a group of people who share the same ancestors, customs, and laws

Chapter 3

Gathering Materials

Indians of the Northwest Coast gathered wood from nearby forests to build plank houses. The wood was made into beams, posts, poles, and planks.

Many tribes used cedar trees. These trees can grow up to 230 feet (70 m) high. A large tree could supply enough wood to make planks for an entire plank house.

FACT

Builders also used wood from cedar trees to build canoes and totem poles.

cedar trees

canoe—a narrow boat that people
move through the water with paddles

Chapter 4

Preparing the Materials

Preparing the wood for a plank house took many steps. First builders cut down a tree and removed the branches and bark.

Most of the tree was used to make planks. Builders pounded **wedges** into the tree with a stone hammer. The wedges split the wood into long, thin planks.

wedge—an object that has a wide end and a narrow end; wedges are used to cut or split apart objects

Chapter 5

Building a Plank House

After builders gathered materials, they started making the house's **frame**. Builders dug holes and set heavy posts in the ground. They used rope to lift beams onto the posts.

Builders used planks to finish the walls and roof. They attached the planks to the frame with wood pegs.

frame—the basic shape over which a house is built

Chapter 6

Inside a Plank House

Most plank houses had an area in the center with a fire pit. Tribes used the fires to cook. The fires also provided heat and light.

Each family had its own space along the walls in a plank house. A family area included a wide bench. People slept and sat on the benches.

Plank houses had places to cook, sleep, and store supplies.

Chapter 7

Plank House Villages

Indians of the Northwest Coast built their plank houses in rows. Small villages were made up of one row of plank houses. Larger villages had several rows of plank houses.

Tribes often built their villages near the Pacific Ocean or along rivers. They built canoes and used them to travel on the water.

Some of the largest villages were made up of as many as 80 houses. Each house could hold as many as 100 people.

Chapter 8

Special Plank Houses

Each village had special plank houses. People gathered at some of these plank houses for **ceremonies**.

Villages also had special plank houses called sweat houses. People poured water onto hot rocks to make steam. The low ceiling of the sweat house kept the steam inside. A sweat house was a place for teaching, storytelling, and singing.

Sweat houses were also used for spiritual purposes.

ceremony—formal actions, words, and often music performed to mark an important occasion

Decorations

Many American Indian tribes on the Northwest Coast decorated their plank houses. They painted images of animals, birds, and people on the outside of their homes.

Some people carved totem poles. Each animal and human form on a totem pole had a special meaning. American Indians on the Northwest Coast still carve totem poles today.

Colorful totem poles are a part of many plank houses.

Amazing but True

Some Northwest Coast tribes were known for special talents. The Haida carved designs into the posts and beams of their plank houses. The Tlingit were known for the decorations on the inside of their homes. The Chinook were famous for their horn carvings. They used the horns of mountain goats and bighorn sheep.

Glossary

canoe (kuh-NOO)—a narrow boat that people move through the water with paddles

ceremony (SER-uh-moh-nee)—formal actions, words, and often music performed to mark an important occasion

frame (FRAYM)—the basic shape over which a house is built

totem pole (TOH-tuhm POHL)—a pole carved and painted with animals and other objects that represent a family

tribe (TRIBE)—a group of people who share the same ancestors, customs, and laws

wedge (WEJ)—an object that has a wide end and a narrow end; wedges are used to cut or split apart objects

Read More

De Capua, Sarah. *The Tlingit.* First Americans. Tarrytown, N.Y.: Marshall Cavendish Benchmark, 2010.

Sonneborn, Liz. *Northwest Coast Indians.* First Nations of North America. Chicago: Heinemann Library, 2012.

Internet Sites

FactHound offers a safe, fun way to find Internet sites related to this book. All of the sites on FactHound have been researched by our staff.

Here's all you do:

Visit *www.facthound.com*

Type in this code: 9781491420553

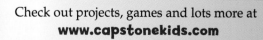

Check out projects, games and lots more at
www.capstonekids.com

Critical Thinking Using the Common Core

1. Look at the photo on page 17. What does it show? Would you like to live in a village like this? Explain why or why not. (Integration of Knowledge and Ideas)

2. A sweat house was a special kind of plank house. What made it special? (Key Ideas and Details)

Index